the FIFTH AMENDMENT today

he 5th AMENDMENT today

Three Speeches by

ERWIN N. GRISWOLD

Dean and Langdell Professor of Law

Harvard Law School

HARVARD UNIVERSITY PRESS · CAMBRIDGE · 1955

Distributed in Great Britain by
Geoffrey Cumberlege, Oxford University Press, London

Library of Congress Catalogue Card Number 55-6809

Printed in the United States of America

PREFACE

The material in this little book is not presented as a scholarly essay. Each of the three chapters was originally prepared for and delivered as a speech, and they are reproduced here in substantially their original form.

The problems with which these speeches are concerned are difficult ones, of vital concern to our society today as they have often been in the past. They involve deep emotions, and it is not always easy to consider them dispassionately. To me, the arguments presented here are conservative arguments, following naturally from the principles on which this country was founded. I have confidence that we will come to right conclusions about these questions today, if we will discuss them fully and frankly and as free from emotions as possible. My purpose in giving the speeches, and in making them available now for wider distribution, has been to contribute to that consideration and discussion.

The first of these speeches was delivered before the Massachusetts Bar Association at its mid-winter meeting in Springfield, Massachusetts, on February 5, 1954. The second speech was given as the Phi Beta Kappa address at Mount Holyoke College, in South Hadley, Massachusetts, on March 24, 1954. The third speech was given twice, first as the Edwin C. Caffrey Memorial Lecture before the New Jersey Institute for Practicing Lawyers, in Newark, New Jersey, on October 14, 1954, and second before the Connecticut Bar Association, in Hartford, Connecticut, on October 19, 1954.

In the preparation of each of the speeches I had the benefit of the advice and suggestions of my colleagues, Livingston Hall and David F. Cavers, for which I want to give acknowledgment and sincere thanks.

ERWIN N. GRISWOLD

Cambridge, Massachusetts

Contents

the FIFTH AMENDMENT today

THE FIFTH AMENDMENT

TO THE CONSTITUTION OF THE UNITED STATES

No person shall be held to answer for a capital, or otherwise infamous crime, unless on a presentment or indictment of a Grand Jury, except in cases arising in the land or naval forces, or in the Militia, when in actual service in time of War or public danger; nor shall any person be subject for the same offence to be twice put in jeopardy of life or limb; *nor shall be compelled in any criminal case to be a witness against himself*, nor be deprived of life, liberty, or property, without due process of law; nor shall private property be taken for public use, without just compensation.

I THE FIFTH AMENDMENT

Old friends are good friends. Yet even with the best of friends problems sometimes arise. I have the feeling that that is in a sense the situation we find ourselves in with respect to the Fifth Amendment. It has been with us a long time. It is rather comforting to have around. Yet in the past few years it has come to our consciousness as it rarely has before, and it has been troublesome to many members of the public. It has seemed to me worth while, therefore, to undertake a review of the Fifth Amendment with the thought that ordinarily the better we understand something in human experience, the less fearsome it becomes.

Before going further it may be well to introduce our old friend itself. The Fifth Amendment contains a number of provisions which are commonplace. It is the source of our constitutional rule that serious criminal charges must be made by indictment of a grand jury. It provides that no person shall be twice put in jeopardy for the same offense, that no person shall be deprived of life, liberty or property without due process of law, and that private property shall not be taken for public use without just compensation. Along with these other provisions is the phrase which has currently come to the fore: "No person . . . shall be compelled in any criminal case to be a witness against himself." Similar provisions have long been included in the constitutions of nearly every state. We are not dealing with either an alien or a novel doctrine.

Historians can trace the origin of this privilege back to the twelfth century. Apparently it began in controversies between the king and the bishops. The bishops sought to examine people about a wide variety of alleged offenses, and the king sought to limit the bishops to purely ecclesiastical subjects. By the sixteenth century the idea had been reduced to a Latin maxim which was rather frequently voiced, but which does not seem by any means to have reflected the practice of that period. This maxim is *Nemo tenetur prodere se ipsum*—or, in English, No one should be required to accuse himself. As early as 1589, the young Coke apparently obtained a writ of prohibition against proceedings in the spiritual courts, on this ground. *Cullier and Cullier*, Cro. Eliz. 201 (1589). But the maxim was then little more than an idea. Over the next fifty years, it was apparently standard practice not only to make suspected persons give evidence against themselves, but also to use torture to make sure that the accused would speak. Indeed, it appears that Coke himself at times participated in the administration of torture for this purpose. As we think of the development of the privilege as it has continued to this day, we should not overlook the fact of its close connection with the struggle to eliminate torture as a governmental practice.

It seems quite clear that we owe the privilege of today primarily to "Freeborn John" Lilburne. He was a cantankerous person, the sort to whom we owe much for many of our basic rights. One of his contemporaries said that "if all the world was emptied of all but John Lilburne, Lilburne would quarrel with John and John with Lilburne." Like most contentious people, he was stubborn. In 1637, he was haled before the Star Chamber on a charge of having imported certain heretical and seditious books. He refused to take the oath to answer truly, and the Council of the Star Chamber condemned him to be whipped and pilloried, for his "boldness in refusing to take a legal oath," without which many offenses might go "undiscovered and unpunished." And in 1638 the sentence was carried out.

But Lilburne persisted. He filed a petition with Parliament, and in 1641 the House of Commons voted that the sentence was "illegal and against the liberty of the subject." Later, the House of Lords concurred with this view, and ordered an indemnity paid to him in the amount of £3,000, which was a very large sum in those days.

This event seems to have been enough to establish the privilege against self-incrimination as a part of the common law. By the latter half of the seventeenth century, we find many occasions when the privilege was recognized by the English courts, and it has been recognized ever since. Indeed, it is still a matter of common law in England. But it is very deeply imbedded in the common law.

Thus, the privilege came to this continent as a part of the legal heritage of our early settlers. Some trace of the privilege is found in Massachusetts as early as 1637, in the trials of Anne Hutchinson and John Wheelwright. For example, a contemporaneous account of Wheelwright's trial contains the following passage: "He demanded whether he were sent for as an innocent person, or as guilty? It was answered neither, but as suspected onely; Then he demanded, who were his accusers? It was answered, his Sermon; (which was there in Court) being acknowledged by himselfe they might thereupon proceed, *ex officio:* at this word great exception was taken, as if the Court intended the course of the High Commission." * The High Commission was, of course, the Star Chamber.

The privilege was also recognized in the other colonies, although the evidences are rather scarce. For one clear case, however, let me read to you a record which has come down to us from Pennsylvania in 1689. In that year, William Bradford was summoned before the Governor and Council of the Province of Pennsylvania. Bradford was the man who introduced the art of print-

* *Short Story of the Rise, Reign, and Ruine of the Antinomians, Familists & Libertines that Infected the Churches of New England,* London, 1644.

ing to the middle provinces of America. He was about twenty-six years old when this episode occurred.

At the instance of one of the citizens of Pennsylvania, Bradford had printed the Charter of the Provinces so that people could see their rights. He had not put his name on the pamphlet, apparently anticipating some trouble. Here is the examination, chiefly by the Governor. You may want to consider whether you have ever heard anything like it before.

"*Governour.*—Why, sir, I would know by what power of authority you thus print? Here is the Charter printed!

"*Bradford.*—It was by Governour Penn's encouragement I came to this Province, and by his license I print.

"*Governour.*—What, sir, had you license to print the Charter? I desire to know from you, whether you did print the Charter or not, and who set you to work?

"*Bradford.*—Governour, it is an impracticable thing for any man to accuse himself; thou knows it very well.

"*Governour.*—Well, I shall not much press you to it, but if you were so ingenuous as to confess, it should go the better with you.

"*Bradford.*—Governour, I desire to know my accusers; I think it very hard to be put upon accusing myself.

"*Governour.*—Can you deny that you printed it? I do know you did print it, and by whose directions, and will prove it, and make you smart for it, too, since you are so stubborn.

"*John Hill.*—I am informed that one hundred and sixty were printed yesterday, and that Jos. Growden saith he gave 20*s* for his part towards the printing it.

"*Bradford.*—It's nothing to me, what 'Jos. Growden saith.' Let me know my accusers, and I shall know the better how to make my defence." *

Little is heard about self-incrimination during the eighteenth century. This may well have been because the privilege was generally recognized in the colonies after it had become established as a part of the common law of England. Violation of the privilege did not figure as one of the major grievances of the colonists, although there are occasional references to "Inquisitional Courts," and there was complaint about the roving jurisdiction of the admiralty courts during the controversy over the Stamp Act. The privilege was included in the Virginia Bill of Rights of 1776 drafted by George Mason, and, apparently largely because of its presence there, it made its way, in various forms, into the constitutions of six or seven of the original states. When the Federal Constitution was ratified, a number of the states proposed amendments, and the privilege against self-incrimination was specifically mentioned. Accordingly, it was included in the proposals made by Congress which became the

* See John William Wallace, *An Address Delivered at the Celebration by the New York Historical Society, May 20, 1863, of the Two Hundredth Birthday of Mr. William Bradford*, Albany, 1863, pp. 49–52.

Fifth Amendment in 1791, and it has been there unchanged ever since. It is truly an old friend, with an ancient and I believe useful history.

A good many efforts have been made to rationalize the privilege, to explain why it is a desirable or essential part of our basic law. None of the explanations is wholly satisfactory. I am going to offer my own attempt to express the reason for the Fifth Amendment, and why I think it is a sound provision of our basic laws, both federal and state.

I would like to venture the suggestion that the privilege against self-incrimination is one of the great landmarks in man's struggle to make himself civilized. As I have already pointed out, the establishment of the privilege is closely linked historically with the abolition of torture. Now we look upon torture with abhorrence. But torture was once used by honest and conscientious public servants as a means of obtaining information about crimes which could not otherwise be disclosed. We want none of that today, I am sure. For a very similar reason, we do not make even the most hardened criminal sign his own death warrant, or dig his own grave, or pull the lever that springs the trap on which he stands. We have through the course of history developed a considerable feeling of the dignity and intrinsic importance of the individual man. Even the evil man is a human being.

If a man has done wrong, he should be punished. But

the evidence against him should be produced, and evaluated by a proper court in a fair trial. Neither torture nor an oath nor the threat of punishment such as imprisonment for contempt should be used to compel him to provide the evidence to accuse or to convict himself. If his crime is a serious one, careful and often laborious police work may be required to prove it by other evidence. Sometimes no other evidence can be found. But for about three centuries in the Anglo-American legal system we have accepted the standard that even then we do not compel the accused to provide that evidence. I believe that is a good standard, and that it is an expression of one of the fundamental decencies in the relation we have developed between government and man.

As that old tartar Mr. Justice Stephen J. Field said, "The essential and inherent cruelty of compelling a man to expose his own guilt is obvious to every one, and needs no illustration." And in words which he approved, the privilege is the "result of the long struggle between the opposing forces of the spirit of individual liberty on the one hand and the collective power of the State on the other." *Brown v. Walker*, 161 U.S. 591, 637 (1896).

Where matters of a man's belief or opinions or political views are essential elements in the charge, it may be most difficult to get evidence from sources other than the suspected or accused person himself. Hence, the significance of the privilege over the years has perhaps been greatest in connection with resistance to prosecution for such offenses as heresy or political crimes. In these areas the privilege against self-incrimination has been a protection for freedom of thought and a hindrance to any government which might wish to prosecute for thoughts and opinions alone.

But the privilege is broader than that. It is applicable to any sort of crime, even the most sordid. Don't we go too far in giving this protection to criminals? Isn't the claim of the privilege the clearest sort of proof that the person who claims it is guilty of a crime? This has been asserted by high authority, but I do not believe it is true.

Apart from its expression of our view of civilized governmental conduct, another purpose of the Fifth Amendment is to protect the innocent. But how can a man claim the privilege if he is innocent? How can a man fear he will incriminate himself if he knows he has committed no crime? This may happen in several ways. A simple illustration will show the possibility.

Consider, for example, the case of the man who has killed another in self-defense, or by accident, without design or fault. He has committed no crime, yet his answer to the question whether he killed the man may well incriminate him. At the very least it will in effect shift the burden of proof to him so that he will have to prove his own innocence. Indeed, the privilege against self-incrimination may well be thought of as a companion of our established rule that a man is innocent until he has been proved guilty.

In this connection let me quote from a Supreme Court decision written long before our present troubles. In *Burdick v. United States*, 236 U.S. 79 (1915), Mr. Justice McKenna wrote, "If it be objected that the sensitiveness of Burdick was extreme because his refusal to answer was itself an implication of crime, we answer, not necessarily in fact, not at all in theory of law."

Now let us turn to an area which is closer to that which has recently been of concern. I am going to ask you to assume two sets of facts. You may think that both of the sets of facts are unlikely, and that they do not correspond with any case you have ever heard of. All I ask is that you assume the facts. I am simply putting a hypothetical case; and the facts are not the facts of any specific case.

Here is Case 1. A man is a college teacher. He is an idealist and perhaps slow to recognize realities, as idealists sometimes are. He has a great urge for what he regards as social reform. He is native born, went to American schools, and loves his country despite what he regards as its imperfections. You may not agree with his ideas but you would respect his honesty and sincerity. He believes himself thoroughly attached to the country and the Constitution, and he abhors anything involving force and violence. He is a good teacher and works hard on his subjects. He has always believed that as a good citizen he should be interested in politics. Neither of the established political parties provided what he wanted. In the relatively calm period of the past middle 1930's, on the solicitation of a friend, he went to a communist meeting and soon joined the Communist Party. At that time the Communist Party was perfectly legal, and regularly appeared on our ballot. He thought he was simply joining a political party. One of the reasons that led him to join was that he regarded fascism as highly immoral and a great danger to the world, and he felt that the communists were fighting fascism in Spain at this time. His interest was not merely in protecting Spain, but, because the danger which many men then feared most was that of the spread of fascism, he thought that fighting fascism in Spain was an important means of guarding against such a danger here.

Now you may say that this is all very unlikely. To this I reply that I am, for the moment, only assuming a hypothetical case, and I should be able to assume any hypothetical case I want. So these are the facts I put before you. You may feel that such a man must have been very naive or lacking in intelligence. To that I would make two replies: First, that conclusion rests on a large amount of hindsight. A man's actions at any time should be evaluated on the basis of the facts then available to him, and the state of his own mind — on the basis of what he actually knew, and not by facts we learn later that were not known to him. And my second reply would be that the man may have been naive or obtuse. I would say that he was at least misguided and unwise. But I would point out that being obtuse or naive is a very different thing from being a traitor or a spy.

Let me add a few more facts, assumed by me as before. Our teacher was in a communist cell, with other teachers. The communists had great plans for this group. They wanted to use it to infiltrate American education. However, the communist command was canny. They knew that many or all of the members of this cell of teachers were politically innocent, and that they would recoil quickly from any proposals for sabotage or the use of force and violence. So they treated this group with great care. The group was never subjected to the rigors of communist discipline. It was a study group, and its discussions were kept on a high intellectual plane. The more sordid features of the communist doctrine were kept thoroughly in the background. Our teacher never engaged in espionage or sabotage or anything like that, and never saw or heard of any such activities by any member of his group. He would have been horrified by any such actions.

Nevertheless, there were things from time to time which he did not like. He rationalized them in various ways: nothing can be perfect; the thing to do is to stay inside and work against excesses; and so on. Besides, he was a stubborn fellow. Once having started out on something he thought was good, he did not lightly give it up. But he became troubled; and after the war he slowly drifted away from the group. He never formally resigned. He just turned away. By the time of the Korean invasion in 1950, he was thoroughly disgusted and saw that he had been used as a dupe. But he was also convinced in his own heart of the rectitude of his actions, if not of their wisdom; and he did not doubt that many of the people who had been associated with him in the venture were just as innocent of wrongdoing as he was sure he was.

Remember, I am doing the assuming. You may feel that these facts do not fit an actual case. But I am not trying to state an actual case. I am just assuming a hypothetical case, which is one of the ancient rights of any law teacher.

Now let me turn to Case 2. This man is also a college teacher. He never joined the Communist Party. He never thought of joining the Communist Party. He knew a good deal about the realities of communism, and he was thoroughly opposed to it. He was, however, a man who was interested in causes. His father had been a minister, who had dedicated his life to helping people. He himself had a great urge to participate in activities which he felt would help to alleviate suffering or contribute to social progress. In fact he was a sucker for almost any kind of an appeal. He contributed modest amounts to China Relief. He had always had a warm feeling for the Chinese. Sometimes he found himself on some of the letterheads of some of these organizations as a sponsor. He was not sure that he remembered giving permission to use his name this way; but the cause, as indicated by the attractive name of the organization, was one that appealed to him, and he did not bother himself much about it. After a while he heard some rumblings that there might be some communist influence in these organizations, but he was slow to believe that that could be true. In some of the organizations, he had been on committees with thoroughly respectable fellow citizens. He did not want to pull out, because he felt that this would let his friends down. Eventually he heard that some of these organizations had been ruled to be subversive by the Attorney General. But he, too, was a stubborn fellow. He believed in the stated objectives of these organizations. He was also a freeborn American, proud of his country's great traditions, and he allowed his name to be used by some of these organizations, as has been said in a recent article, "as a gesture of opposition to the procedure of proscribing organizations without giving them the right to be heard."

Well, that is the end of my assuming. Let us see what happens to these two individuals. Remember that both of these individuals feel that they are innocent of any wrongdoing. Each one is pure in heart, and perhaps a little too certain of his own rectitude. Each one may now regret some of the things he did, but he does not think that they were wrong. Each one is certain that he is morally innocent of any crime.

We can consider Case 1 first. He is the man who was

a member of the Communist Party. He is summoned to appear before a Congressional Committee, and is asked whether he is a communist. He answers truthfully: "No." Then he is asked whether he ever was a communist. He is now surely subjected to a substantial risk, even though he honestly believes that he has committed no crime. He knows that a number of communists have been convicted under the Smith Act of 1940, and more have been indicted. Our teacher perhaps magnifies his own predicament. He sees the jail doors opening up if he himself gives the evidence that he was once a communist. Interestingly enough, Section 4(f) of the Internal Security Act of 1950 (commonly known as the McCarran Act) provides specifically that "neither the holding of office nor membership in any communist organization by any person shall constitute per se a violation of . . . this section or of any other criminal statute." But this was enacted after his period of Party membership. It has been declared to be a crime to be a communist in Massachusetts since 1951, but there may be some possible room to question the effectiveness of this statute in view of the provision of the federal Act.

After much internal torment, the witness finally decides to claim the privilege of the Fifth Amendment with respect to the question of his past membership in the Communist Party. Putting aside the question of his wisdom in doing this, can there be any doubt that the claim is legally proper? Past membership in the Communist Party is not a crime in itself; but admitting such membership may well be a link in a chain of proof of a criminal charge against him. Persons have been prosecuted under the Smith Act for membership in the Communist Party plus something else. If he supplies the proof of his own membership in the Party, he does not know what other evidence may then be brought against him to show that he has committed a crime. Thus, an answer to the question will definitely incriminate him, that is, provide evidence which could be used in a prosecution against him. Yet, remember that he thoroughly believes that he is not guilty of any crime; and on the facts I have given he is not guilty of a crime.

There are other factors that influence his conclusion. His own experience is an ordeal. He does not want his friends to be subjected to it. He believes in their innocence of any crime. If he thought that they had committed crimes, he would promptly tell the proper officers of the government. By claiming the privilege against self-incrimination, he can refrain from naming any of his associates. He feels a strong sense of loyalty to them. He feels a strong sense of loyalty to his country, too; but since he is convinced that neither he nor his associates have in fact done anything wrong, his desire to protect them from having to experience his own predicament seems to him to have prevailing weight in the actual circumstances.

He claims the privilege. He cannot be prosecuted on the basis of any evidence he has provided. There can be no doubt, I believe, that his claim of privilege is legally justified. Yet, note that on the facts I have assumed he is not guilty of any crime. Of course his claim of privilege as to his membership in the Communist Party means that he must also claim the privilege as to all other questions which relate in any way to what he did, or to his associates in the activity. For if he answers any of those questions, it will clearly connote his own communist activity.

There is one small point which might be brought in here. It is sometimes said that the privilege may only be rightly claimed if the answer to the incriminating question would be "Yes." I do not believe that is true. Our man in Case 1 has testified that he is not now a communist. He claims the privilege as to a question which asks him if he ever was a member of the Communist Party. He is then asked: "When did you cease to be a member?" He must claim the privilege as to this, or else his answer will disclose that he once was a member, as to which he has legitimately claimed the privilege. Then the examiner starts a new line. He says: "Were you a member of the Communist Party yesterday?" Now the answer is "No." But the witness who has taken this line cannot answer that question. For if he does, the questions will be continued: "Were you a member of the Party last year? — two years ago? — three years ago?" If he answers any of these accurately with a "No," he will come to the place where he must claim the privilege if he is to maintain his basic position. In this way, the date of his withdrawal could be pinpointed, thus giving valuable information for a possible prosecution. Moreover, he may not be sure just when he withdrew; it was a gradual process. And he may have legitimate fears that an honest answer he might give to a question relating to the transitional period might get him involved in a prosecution for perjury. At any rate, it seems clear that questions of this sort are an illustration of a type of question as to which the privilege may be legitimately claimed, as far as the law is concerned, even though the answer to the question would be "No."

Let us turn to Case 2, which we can dispose of briefly. You will remember that that was the man who had lent his name to causes, and had contributed money; and the causes have now turned out to be communist fronts, although they were attractively named, and many good Americans were, at one time or another, associated with them. But he was never a member of the Communist Party.

This man likewise is summoned before a Congressional Investigating Committee. The mere fact that he is summoned shows that he is suspected of something rather serious, and he is badly worried. He is asked whether he is now a member of the Communist Party; and he answers "No." Then he is asked whether he ever was in the past. The answer is in fact "No," as we have seen. But he is now in great fear. If he says: "No," then he may be subjecting himself to a real risk of a prosecution for perjury. He may rightly fear that proof of the fact of his joining and contributing to so many agencies which have turned out to be front organizations might lead a jury to believe that he actually was a communist.

Now it is probably true that fear of a prosecution for perjury for an answer given to a question is not a proper basis for a claim of the privilege. If it was, almost any witness could claim the privilege as to any question. But our man is in a somewhat different situation. If he says "No" to the question of communist membership, then in his own interest he may have to undertake to state and explain his membership and activities in the various front organizations. The net result may be that he will have to give much evidence which could be used against him in an attempt to prove that he was a member of the communist conspiracy. It would appear, therefore, that he can properly claim the privilege even though his answer to the question as to Communist Party membership at any time would honestly and rightly be "No."

In both of the cases I have put, the privilege may be claimed although the individual was guilty of no crime. In the second case it may be claimed although the person was never a member of the Communist Party. In each case, there may be a "natural" inference from the claim of the privilege, and in each case that inference would in fact be unwarranted. The claim of the privilege is surely a serious business, but it is equally surely not the equivalent of an admission of criminal conduct.

There are other reasons why a person may claim the privilege in a particular case. He might get bad advice; but I do not want to press that, as I think that in many of these cases the individual's troubles are caused in part by the fact that he chooses to make his own decisions and does not accept sound advice. But we should not forget that a person on the witness stand may be badly frightened, even though he is wholly innocent. For example, the Supreme Court of the United States has said, in *Wilson v. United States,* 149 U.S. 60, 66 (1893):

"It is not every one who can safely venture on the witness stand though entirely innocent of the charge against him. Excessive timidity, nervousness when facing others and attempting to explain transactions of a suspicious character, and offences charged against him, will often confuse and embarrass him to such a degree as to increase rather than remove prejudices against him. It is not every one, however honest, who would, therefore, willingly be placed on the witness stand."

A witness lost in fear and confusion might turn to the privilege as a means of sanctuary from a situation which he feels himself incompetent to handle. Consider also how much the chance of a witness losing his calm and collected demeanor is enhanced by such things as television, radio microphones, movie cameras, flashing flash bulbs, and procedures which may not seem to him to be based upon the finest spirit of fairness. In connection with this I might mention the recent decision of the United States Court of Appeals for the Sixth

Circuit in *Aiuppa v. United States*, 201 F.2d 287, 300 (1952), where we find the following language in the opinion:

"But, in concluding, we think it may not be amiss to say that, notwithstanding the pronouncements of the committee chairman as to intended fairness, the courts of the United States could not emulate the committee's example and maintain even a semblance of fair and dispassionate conduct of trials in criminal cases.

"Despite the enjoyment by millions of spectators and auditors of the exhibition by television of the confusion and writhings of widely known malefactors and criminals, when sharply questioned as to their nefarious activities, we are unable to give judicial sanction, in the teeth of the Fifth Amendment, to the employment by a committee of the United States Senate of methods of examination of witnesses constituting a triple threat: answer truly and you have given evidence leading to your conviction for a violation of federal law; answer falsely and you will be convicted of perjury; refuse to answer and you will be found guilty of criminal contempt and punished by fine and imprisonment. In our humble judgment, to place a person not even on trial for a specified crime in such predicament is not only not a manifestation of fair play, but is in direct violation of the Fifth Amendment to our national Constitution."

Ordinarily when the privilege of the Fifth Amendment is exercised, it is in a criminal trial. There a specific charge has been made, and the prosecution has by evidence established a prima facie case of guilt of the particular crime charged in the complaint or indictment. Under such circumstances there is much more than the mere claim of the privilege on which to rest an inference of guilt.

In investigations, however, there are no carefully formulated charges. Evidence to support such charges has not been introduced and made known to the witness before he is called upon to answer. He has no opportunity for cross-examination of other witnesses, and often little or no opportunity to make explanations which might have a material bearing on the whole situation. In the setting of an investigation, therefore, the basis for the inference from a claim of privilege against self-incrimination is much less than it is when the privilege is exercised in an ordinary criminal trial.

There are two more matters to which I should like to make brief reference. The first of these is the rather technical legal doctrine known as waiver of the privilege. A clear instance of waiver occurs when a defendant in a criminal case voluntarily takes the stand. He then becomes subject to cross-examination, and must answer relevant questions. So far as witnesses at investigations are concerned, our current learning on this is based largely on the Supreme Court's decision in *Rogers v. United States*, 340 U.S. 367 (1951). In that case, a witness testified that she had been treasurer of a local communist party, had had possession of the records, and had turned them over to another person. She then declined to name the person to whom she had given them, claiming the privilege under the Fifth Amendment. The Supreme Court held that by giving the testimony she did she had waived the privilege, and that she was guilty of contempt for refusing to answer the further quesitons. There was a dissenting opinion by Justices Black, Frankfurter, and Douglas.

My own view is that this decision was not soundly reasoned, and that it has led to unfortunate results. To me the analogy of an adversary proceeding is not apt when applied to an investigation. As a consequence of this case, witnesses who have legitimate fears of prosecution, but who might be willing to cooperate as far as they could, are induced (if not actually compelled) to refuse to answer any questions at all. For if they do answer a single question, it may be contended that they have waived the privilege so that thereafter they may be compelled to testify against themselves. This threat of waiver is not an imaginary matter. It may be found frequently in the transcripts of the proceedings of Congressional committees.

My guess as to the law is that the *Rogers* case applies only where the witness has given an incriminating answer to a prior question. I do not think it would apply if a witness was asked if he had been a member of the Communist Party in 1945, and he said "No." By the latter answer he has not opened up anything which he refuses to explain. Nevertheless, it will take a Supreme Court decision to provide this clarification of the *Rogers* case; and counsel advising a client may well hesitate to make his client bear the risk and expense of taking a case all the way to the Supreme Court. With the *Rogers* case on the books, the only safe advice may be to claim the privilege at the earliest possible moment, so as to be sure to avoid a charge of waiver.

This doctrine of waiver is, I believe, the true explanation of the refusal of some witnesses to answer such questions as "Have you ever taught communist doctrine in your classroom?" or "Have you ever solicited students to join the Communist Party?" These refusals have been deeply disturbing to the public. Yet, the answer to these questions may be "No"; but the witness nevertheless fears that he cannot give that answer without its being said that he has waived the privilege as to questions about other sorts of communist activity. Here again we have a situation where the obvious inference from the refusal to answer the question may be completely unwarranted.

Finally, I would like to make reference to one more problem which is collateral to that of the Fifth Amendment. Suppose a witness is summoned before an investigating committee. He does not claim a privilege against self-incrimination, and talks freely about himself, answering all questions about his own activity. He takes the position, however, that he will not answer questions about others. Or suppose a person first refuses to answer virtually all questions, claiming the Fifth Amendment privilege, but he later decides to waive the privilege as to himself. However, he refuses as a matter which he regards as one of principle to identify other persons. What should be the situation with respect to such a person?

There have been a number of people who have been summoned before investigating committees and taken this position from the outset. They have answered all questions about themselves, and have refused to identify others. As far as I know, no academic person who has done this has been cited for contempt; nor has any such person lost his job. Should it be any different where the witness has first relied on the Fifth Amendment, but has later changed his position, waiving the privilege as to himself, but still refusing to answer as to others?

The problem is undeniably a difficult one. So long as the witness was claiming the privilege, it could be argued that he had done no wrong. If he had committed any crime, the evidence should be brought forth in the proper way and tried out in court. His refusal to answer was not evidence of any crime. This argument, however, is not available where he waives the privilege but refuses to answer questions relating to other persons. Then his Fifth Amendment privilege is wholly gone, and his situation presents new and rather different problems.

Whether he has committed a crime by his refusal to testify may be extremely difficult to tell. Even if he is cited by the legislative body, it will still be for the grand jury to decide whether to indict; it will remain to the courts to decide such questions as whether the committee was properly constituted, and whether the question asked was relevant to the inquiry. We should not forget that a prosecution for contempt was set aside within the past year by the Supreme Court on the ground that the questions asked the witness — as to the identity of his contributors — were not relevant to the particular inquiry. *United States v. Rumeley*, 345 U.S. 41 (1953).

However such questions go, though, would it not seem that such a person is at least in no worse a position morally than he was when he stood on the Fifth Amendment? He should not be worse off for being willing to speak fully and frankly about himself than he was when he would not talk at all. His refusal to tell on his friends may be both contrary to valid law and unwise. Nevertheless, it may be based on strong grounds of conscience.

Let me do a little more assuming: Let us assume that the witness feels positive in his own mind that the persons with whom he was associated did no wrong to our country. They did not engage in espionage or sabotage or anything like that. They were merely hopeful but misguided people, as he was. Let us assume, too, that this is all far in the past. The persons in question are in other work. They have families to support. If their names are disclosed, they will surely lose their jobs. He must then resolve for himself the question whether he will give their names and subject them to the same sort of ordeal he has been through in order to save himself from further difficulty and possible prosecution. He may be wrong if he decides that he should not protect himself by sacrificing them. I recognize the legal obligation to testify as to others, and the general importance of this both in trials and in investigations. But can it be said clearly that his action is always immoral?

Of course he may be wrong in his judgment of these other people. They may be worse than he thinks they are. But we all have to use judgment on such things. A man may honestly feel that he cannot bring suffering to others in order to save himself. To a considerable extent such questions can only be resolved in a man's own conscience. We are a society which has long depended on and applauded the virtues of the rugged individualist.

I do not justify the past or present conduct of anyone. I seek only to explain. Because some members of university faculties have claimed privilege under the Fifth Amendment and refused to answer questions, many members of the general public have come to have fear of our educational institutions and general mistrust of academic people. I firmly believe that these fears are unwarranted. I have tried here to show how some of the things that have happened could have happened without there being anything rotten in the universities. It may be a serious error of judgment for an academic person to claim the privilege of the Fifth Amendment, or to refuse to answer questions; but the conduct, regrettable as it is, does not show the existence of treason, espionage, sabotage, or any other serious crime.

The great misfortune from all this, I believe, is that charges are made against our universities and other educational institutions, and more or less believed by some segments of our people. I think myself that it is easy to overestimate the extent of that belief, but it cannot be denied that there is disagreement, uneasiness, and even fear in some quarters. As I have said, I think these fears are not soundly based. It is an injustice not only to the faculty members of our great universities but to the country to allow any conclusion to stand that they are not good Americans or that they do not serve their country well.

As conservative a judge as Pierce Butler once wrote:

"It has always been recognized in this country, and it is well to remember, that few if any of the rights of the people guarded by fundamental law are of greater importance to their happiness and safety than the right to be exempt from all unauthorized, arbitrary or unreasonable inquiries and disclosures in respect of their personal and private affairs." (*Sinclair v. United States*, 279 U.S. 135, 178; 1927.)

On this matter some final observations may be in order, based on our traditional practices and rules. In our criminal courts, we would never think of requiring an accused person to answer questions. He doesn't have to take the stand at all, and if he does do so, he has the protection of an impartial judge, and the right to have his counsel speak in court in his behalf.

Why should it be so different in a legislative inquiry, when the information that is sought relates to the witness' own conduct? I recognize fully the power of the Senate and the House of Representatives, the lineal descendants of the Houses of Parliament. These are deliberative bodies, and all points of view are usually represented among their members. Their actions are taken after debate, and represent the judgment of many people from all parts of the country.

I recognize also that these bodies have to operate through committees. A committee in the common acceptance of the term is a group of persons, usually appointed to represent various points of view. Its actions reflect collective judgment taken after consideration and deliberation. In this light, I ask a question: Should these broad investigative powers ever be held by a single person, even though he is formally clothed with the title of a sub-committee?

The more I think about this, the more it seems to me to be an unsound practice. There is nothing about the nature of membership in the Senate or the House of Representatives which should give each member a general commission to go through the length and breadth of the land, far from his own state or district, far from the seat of the general government, making inquiry about any subject, even on formal delegation to him from his

House or one of its committees. Committees I am willing to accept. Sub-committees of one give me pause. It may well be that only the Houses of Congress can effectively deal with this problem, but I respectfully commend it to them for their consideration.

And so I come back where I started. The privilege against self-incrimination embodied in the Fifth Amendment has been a long time with us. It is, I believe, a good friend as well as an old friend. It embodies a sound value which we should preserve. As we increase our understanding of it, and the part it has long played in protecting the individual against the collective power of the state, we will have better appreciation of some of the basic problems of our time.

2 PER LEGEM TERRAE

Per Legem Terrae means, of course, "By the Law of the Land." What is the significance of those words today? A few weeks ago I spoke on the subject of the Fifth Amendment's provision against requiring a man to incriminate himself. It is my plan now to talk about another fundamental idea which has its roots in the distant past and which has become a vital and pervading part of our Anglo-American legal heritage.

These words which I have chosen as the title of my speech go back to Magna Carta, the Great Charter of 1215, wrested from King John by his barons, and the source of ideas far more potent than they could have realized. For the barons were interested in protecting themselves against an overbearing King, and had little interest in the basic rights of common men. In the thirty-ninth article of Magna Carta, apparently taken from an earlier Continental source, they included the provision that "No freeman shall be taken and imprisoned or disseised or exiled or in any way destroyed, nor will we go upon him nor send upon him, except by the lawful judgment of his peers and by the law of the land." "By the law of the land" — these are the words with which we now render the Latin of the original, "per legem terrae." The phrase has had an almost unexampled persistence and power. Professor McIlwain has said that "chapter thirty-nine was in 1215 the most important chapter in the charter, as it is today." ("Due Process of Law in Magna Carta," 14 *Columbia L. Rev.* 41; 1914.)

Thus there was planted in the stream of English law and English history — a stream of which ours is now the largest branch — the seed of a great idea, an idea which has made an incalculable contribution to the development of our institutions. Just a few words, but they have time and again arisen at critical moments of our history, and in one way or another have contributed to that long course of events through which we have sought to make ourselves civilized.

Do I not exaggerate? "By the law of the land" — can these words have such great significance? Are they not merely procedural at best? Historians have long debated the exact meaning of the various clauses in Magna Carta. A leading author has said that what the barons "wished to secure was justice and legality in all of the king's actions affecting private rights." (Mott, *Due Process of Law*, 1926, p. 36.)

We have seen how and when the idea was planted. How did it grow? In the next century, a statute of Edward III made it clear that the protection of the article applied to all men without limitation — "of what estate or condition that he be." 28 Edward III, c. 3 (1354). And it was this same statute of Edward III that first used the phrase which has become commonplace in our own history, for he said that no man should be harmed in any way except "by due process of law." This first appearance of the phrase was actually in the Law French of that time — "par due process de ley."

Over the next three hundred years, many men, at many times, appealed to the Great Charter and the conceptions which it embodied. For our purposes, we may move on to Lord Coke, the great figure of the first part of the seventeenth century.

In an outstanding event of the history of our liberties, Coke advanced "the law of the land" against the king. This was in 1608 when James the First asserted that he had power to take such cases as he might be pleased to determine and decide them as if he were himself a judge. Coke opposed this royal claim, and the king was greatly offended, saying that if Coke's view were sound, then the king was "under the law, which was treason to affirm." To this Coke replied in words which he took from Bracton, that the king "ought not to be under men but under God and the law." *Prohibitions del Roy*, 12 Rep. 63b, 65a (1608). This was a crucial application of the basic idea which we are considering tonight. These words, I am proud to say, are inscribed in their original Latin — *Non sub Homine sed sub Deo et Lege* — over the portal of the Harvard Law School.

In 1628, Coke wrote a Commentary on Magna Carta,

as a part of the work that is known as his Institutes. He showed the identity in meaning between the two phrases "the law of the land" and "due process of law," and that the purpose of these provisions was to protect the subject from oppressive uses of authority. In his words: "Every oppression against law, by colour of any usurped authority is a kinde of destruction, . . . : and it is the worst oppression that is done by the colour of justice." (Coke, *Second Institutes,* 1656, p. 48.) In this and other passages from his Institutes, Coke interpreted Magna Carta not so much in the light of its own historical setting as in the light and for the purposes of his own time.

Coke was a member of the committee that drew up the Petition of Right, in 1628, and was probably its principal author. In this document the House of Commons asserted itself against King Charles by condemning arbitrary taxation and imprisonment, and the billeting of soldiers, all as being contrary to the law of the land.

Out of all of these events there grew a great revival of the idea of protection of the citizen inherent in the phrases "law of the land" and "due process of law." This is perhaps most strikingly shown in the fact that the Act of Parliament which finally abolished the Star Chamber in 1640 recited that the actions of that body had not been in accordance with "due process of law," and were contrary to the "law of the land." Much of Locke's political writing was based on the ideas embodied in these two phrases. Both Coke and Locke had great influence on the development of the ideas of the colonists in this country a hundred years later.

These ideas came to America as a part of the heritage of our early English settlers, and we had here a soil on which they could flourish. When James Otis made his great argument in the "Writs of Assistance" case, Quincy 51 (1761), he included an argument based on Magna Carta, with specific reference to the "law of the land" provision. This argument had great influence on the colonial pamphleteers who had so much to do with the mobilization of public opinion in the period. John Adams was one of those who took up this idea. The argument that "taxation without representation is tyranny" was simply an application of the basic idea of due process of law, thought by the colonists to be established by Magna Carta and thus to be their birthright.

When, after the Revolution, and the successful adoption of the Federal Constitution, it was decided to add a Bill of Rights to that Constitution, it was natural that this traditional right should be included. The Fifth Amendment, largely drafted by James Madison, includes a provision that "No person shall . . . be deprived of life liberty or property without due process of law." Thus has the great provision of Magna Carta been carried forward to our own fundamental law. As Dr. Mott has said, "This portion of the Fifth Amendment may thus be regarded as containing phraseology of purest gold mined under the stress of heated constitutional crises, refined by the fire of violent revolutions, proved by the acid test of centuries of struggle, and molded by the hand of one of America's greatest constitutional draftsmen." (Mott, *Due Process of Law*, 1926, p. 18.)

And thus we have this ancient doctrine included in our Constitution — now in both the Fifth and the Fourteenth Amendments. What the barons did in 1215, what Coke and his associates did in the seventeenth century, what the American patriots did in the eighteenth century — all of this and much more provides a clear continuity, linking our present institutions closely with all the struggles for liberty in the past three quarters of a millennium.

But is not the due process clause technical lawyers' stuff? Was it not on the basis of the due process clause that the Supreme Court held that New York could not fix the length of hours that bakers might work, and that Congress could not fix a minimum wage for women in the District of Columbia? What do such decisions have to do with the struggle to obtain and to maintain liberty? The answer I would give is: Very little. They are only eddies in the stream which carries on the great idea. For the idea of due process, of "the law of the land" is a great idea, and one of our greatest heritages from the past. It is something of the spirit, something that gives life to our political institutions. In very large part we take it for granted in our day-to-day relations with our fellow men and with the several governments with which we deal. It is so deeply ingrained in us all that it is rarely violated; and many of the violations which do occur are naturally of the more or less technical sort with which courts deal.

In the long run, ideas are more powerful than more tangible weapons. And the idea of due process has been a very fruitful and pervading one in our history. What does it mean? Can it be defined? Many people feel the need for a rather precise sort of a definition of concepts with which they deal — but this is not that sort of an idea. This is an idea born out of the hearts of men. It has great capacity for development and growth, and yet a rather clear basic content. Perhaps the essential thought can be put by saying that due process has some application wherever men feel a sense of injustice. Thus it becomes a chief source of support for individual liberties. What is liberty? Is it not freedom or protection of the individual against arbitrary or improper exercise of the organized power of the state? What is a tyrant? Is he not a man who exercises the collective power of the state in an arbitrary, capricious, or purely selfish manner? Such words as "arbitrary" and "capricious" are difficult words. They may not in fact mean much more than "unreasonable," and that in turn may mean in substance "not customary," or not what we are accustomed to. Perhaps it may be said that we are accustomed to decent treatment from our public officers, and that our hearts and minds recoil when that custom is broken. It is with this sort of thing that the idea of due process, of "the law of the land" is concerned.

Violations of cherished ideals and aspirations have often been overcome in our history by arguments based on the general idea of due process, of the law of the land. In recent times, the due process clause has been the basis of decisions on such questions as these: (1) That a judge cannot properly try a case if he is directly interested in the outcome, *Tumey v. Ohio*, 273 U.S. 10 (1927); and (2) That a person cannot be subjected to a secret trial, with no chance to defend himself, *In re Oliver*, 333 U.S. 257 (1948).

Now let us turn to the question which has been constantly recurring in recent days. Does this basic idea have any application to legislative investigations? Do these investigations always measure up to our ideal of due process of law? I think it fair to say that a large section of the public has from time to time felt "a sense of injustice" with respect to some of these hearings; and if they have, then there is a situation where the ancient ideal of due process is involved. A failure to appreciate the intimate relation between sound procedure and the preservation of liberty is implicit, may I say, in that saddest and most short-sighted remark of our times: "I don't like the methods, but . . ." For methods and procedures are of the essence of due process, and are of vital importance to liberty. As Mr. Justice Brandeis wrote some thirty years ago, "In the development of our liberty insistence on procedural regularity has been a large factor." *Burdeau v. McDowell*, 256 U.S. 465, 477 (1921). More recently Mr. Justice Frankfurter has put the same truth in these words: "The history of liberty has largely been the history of observance of procedural safeguards." *McNabb v. United States*, 318 U.S. 332, 347 (1943).

The complaint against the Star Chamber was chiefly one of bad procedures. Torture is a procedure, and inquisition without charge, forcing a witness to testify against himself, and the other things which were standard practice in the infamous Star Chamber would all fall into the category of procedure. Liberty is established and preserved by the development and maintenance of proper procedures. It is, in last analysis, only through procedural rules that the individual is protected against arbitrary governmental action. And, as we have seen, the very essence of liberty is the protection of the individual against arbitrary application of the collective power of the state.

Do not misunderstand me. I am not opposed to legislative investigations. They clearly have a proper place in our governmental structure. The fact, though, that they can be useful and necessary, does not mean that they should not be properly conducted, and under proper safeguards and procedures. Nor does it mean that when not properly conducted they may not violate our basic and fundamental conceptions of due process, rooted so firmly in Magna Carta. In my opinion, for what it is worth, some recent legislative investigations have been clear violations of due process. If so, why have the courts not so held? The answer is easy. The courts do not have the sole responsibility for the proper conduct of our government. As Mr. Justice Stone once said: "Courts are not the only agency of government that must be assumed to have capacity to govern." *United States v. Butler*, 297 U.S. 1, 87 (1936). At this point another important governmental doctrine comes into play — the separation of powers. The courts have their responsibilities, but so do the executive and the legislative branches of the government. All are sworn to uphold the Constitution, including the due process clause of so ancient and vital origin.

The responsibility for the proper conduct of legislative investigations is clearly in the legislature. In the case of investigations by the federal legislature, the responsibility is clearly in Congress and its two Houses. Has this responsibility been fully met? It seems to me quite clear that the answer to that question is No. Why has it not been met? What can be done about it?

Before turning to an answer to those questions, I would like to pause to make one important observation. It is wholly clear, I believe, that no senator or representative has any power whatever to make an investigation, to require the presence of witnesses and their answers to questions, or to do anything of this sort, merely because he is a congressman or senator. An election to the House of Representatives or to the Senate does not make a man any sort of a magistrate, nor does it vest him with any power at all over his fellow citizens except to cast his vote in the body to which he has been elected. The power of investigation is a power which is solely attributable to the collective body, the House of Representatives or the Senate.

Where there is an investigation being conducted, the power that is being exercised is that of the House or the Senate. No committee of either body has any power to conduct any investigation except as a result of a delegation from its House of Congress. No sub-committee of a committee has any power to investigate except on a delegation of the power delegated by the House or Senate to the committee. If there is a sub-committee of one, the power exercised by that one is not any power that is his by virtue merely of his being a member of the legislative body. If he has any power, it is only because there has been a proper delegation or sub-delegation to him of the basic power of the House or Senate.

I mention this because it is important in the consideration of the questions which I have posed, and to which I want to suggest some answers. Since the power exercised by a committee or a sub-committee, or a sub-committee of one, is the power of the House or Senate itself, responsibility for that power and its exercise rests not on the committee or the sub-committee of one or more, but upon the House or Senate itself, acting, of course, by a majority vote of its members. One of the important steps which must be taken if we are to find a solution for problems in this area is, I believe, to focus attention on the fact that these hearings which are the occasion of concern are not merely private frolics of an individual member, but are an exercise of the power of a House of Congress for which every member of that House has a full and equal responsibility.

Clearly there is a problem here. Why has it not been dealt with long before this time? It is a difficult problem, and it would be too much to expect it to be completely solved in a short time. But the fact is that virtually nothing at all has been done about it. There have been earnest efforts in both state and federal legislative bodies to formulate codes or standards of proper procedure in investigations. But the actual results so far are not impressive. Why is that? One reason, I think, is that only recently has it become a serious problem. It is clear that our legislative bodies include a very large number of able, high-minded men, who are just as much interested in the ideal of due process as you and I. Why have they not taken action to establish proper procedures in legislative investigations?

The answer is not simple, but there is one aspect of it which is, I think, perhaps insufficiently understood by the average citizen. The fact is that, for practical purposes, the House of Representatives and the Senate are regarded by their members as clubs — of which the Senate is, of course, the more exclusive. Each member of the House or Senate has his own standards. And in a great many cases these standards are very high. But with almost no exception, no member seeks to impose his standards on any other member. Once you are in the club, how you act is up to you, and no member wants to undertake to interfere in the conduct of any other member — partly, I suppose, because he does not want anyone else to interfere with him. This is unfortunate, I think, though perhaps natural and understandable.

There is an important distinction here, which has, I fear, been overlooked, in the consideration of this matter of legislative investigations. For a Senator or Congressman who is conducting an investigation, either as a subcommittee of one, or in association with other members, is not acting as an individual. Everything he does directly involves the other members of his House, and they should share responsibility for the exercise of the power they have delegated, power which inheres only in the body as a whole. The problem can be solved by establishing by law, or by rule of each House, a proper standard of procedure for the conduct of legislative investigations which will keep them wholly consistent with our basic and deeply felt notions of due process of law.

In the concluding portion of this talk, I would like to outline some provisions which, it seems to me, should be included in an established regulation of procedure of legislative investigations. I have in mind primarily the federal scene. Before turning to that, though, I would like to point out that we are not wholly without precedents. This is, interestingly enough, an area in which the states have, on the whole, done a much better job than has the federal legislature. In New York a commission has recently made a promising report on this whole matter. In Massachusetts, the legislature, in establishing two recent recess commissions, one to investigate crime, and the other to investigate communism, has included substantial provisions designed to protect the rights of witnesses and to insure the proper conduct of these investigations. As a result, there have been few complaints about the activities of these commissions, and we have not been subjected to the spectacles which have so frequently been produced on the federal stage. For these wise provisions we should give respect and thanks to the Massachusetts legislature and to its Committee on the Judiciary which was undoubtedly responsible for their first formulation. I am glad to pay this tribute to our local legislators. But why cannot the federal Congress do as well?

Much work has been done over the past several years toward formulating a suitable and proper code of conduct for federal legislative investigations. A number of members of Congress have devoted much thought and effort to this task, and a number of bills have been introduced. Recently President Eisenhower announced that he understood that Congress was going to establish such standards — and it is clearly the responsibility of Congress. Legislative leadership on this question is still not impressive, but it should come. Probably it would be more accurate to say that there has been leadership and good leadership, but it has been hard so far for the leaders to get an effective following. The matter is too important, too closely connected with our basic liberties, to be longer neglected.

These are some of the things, as I see it, which should be included in a proper Code of Practice for legislative investigations:

1. Of first importance is the elimination of the one-man sub-committee in any proceeding involving a witness who appears involuntarily. In our concern over recent events, we should not forget that there is much of the business of Congress which is not controversial, and there are many situations where a witness wants to appear. As long as he appears voluntarily, there may be little objection, as far as the witness is concerned, to his appearing before any sort of body, including a sub-committee of one. Even then there may be a public interest in having a member of the other party present so that more than one point of view may be represented. When a witness appears under subpoena, when he is compelled to testify against his will, the situation is wholly different. Then I say that the power of Congress against him should not be asserted by a sub-committee of a single member.

2. Closely related to this is the matter of the issuance of subpoenas. The practice with respect to subpoenas has

come to be very loose; indeed it might be called lax. It is the standard practice, I believe, in many committees, for the chairman of the committee to sign up a batch of subpoenas in blank, and hand them to the staff of the committee. Then the staff fills in the name of a witness whose testimony is wanted, and the subpoena is served upon him. Such a practice seems to me to be highly improper.

There is here a close analogy with a search warrant, which can only be issued by a judge. With respect to such warrants, Mr. Justice Douglas has said that the requirement of a search warrant is made "so that an objective mind might weigh the need. . . . The right of privacy was deemed too precious to entrust to the discretion of those whose job is the detection of crime and the arrest of criminals. Power is a heady thing; . . ." *McDonald v. United States*, 335 U.S. 451, 455–456 (1948).

No subpoena should be issued to compel testimony except as a result of the action of the committee itself, not the chairman alone, or its staff. There are few ways in which the organized power of the state is brought to bear on a citizen more sharply than through a subpoena to compel testimony. Such a power should not be exercised on the judgment or discretion or whim of a single man.

3. When a witness is summoned, he should be given several protections which have not heretofore been made available. He should be told in advance the subject and

the scope of the inquiry. He should have the right to counsel, and counsel should be entitled to speak on his behalf as well as to advise him as to his rights.

In many committees now, the right to counsel is formally recognized. But counsel, though present, is restricted to giving advice when called upon. He cannot address the committee; and counsel who have sought to do so have been ejected from hearing rooms. The right should be a right to effective counsel, and not the mere shadow of that right that has been recently allowed.

4. If testimony is taken in executive session (which should never be done unless the witness is willing) no member of the committee or of its staff should make available selected portions of the testimony, or summaries or incomplete versions of it. The committee should not be allowed to say, through its chairman or otherwise, that "we have evidence of" so and so, unless that evidence is produced in an open hearing.

5. Of very great importance, I believe, is a rule protecting the witness from having to submit to broadcasting, television, newsreel cameras, or any other form of recording or reproduction, except the ordinary stenographic transcript. Even flashing flash bulbs can be an indignity and a source of strain to a witness. It is high time that we recognized and accepted the fact that legislative investigations are not a part of show business. Witnesses should not be required to testify in order to provide a spectacle for the public. Requiring testimony under such conditions is not compatible with any sound

notion of due process of law, and I would expect our courts, as some have already done, to uphold a witness who refuses to testify for broadcast of any sort. We have even had Congressional investigations put on with sponsors, with advertising during the intervals. Can anyone possibly defend such a practice?

6. In this connection I would like to state my own view that a legislative investigation is improper when its sole or basic purpose is to "expose" people or to develop evidence for use in criminal prosecutions. We have had chairmen of legislative committees who have announced that that was the purpose of the hearings they were conducting. In my opinion, they have thus demonstrated the impropriety of the exercise of power which they are seeking to carry out, and I would hope that the courts, when properly invoked, would decide that there was no legislative power for such a purpose.

There are many other rights and refinements which should be established and recognized in connection with legislative investigations. For example, a person summoned should have due notice of the nature of the evidence that is wanted from him. A witness should surely be entitled to explain his answers, and he should have an opportunity to answer any charges made against him or any evidence against him produced by other witnesses.

Many congressmen and senators are aware of these problems and are trying to get them worked out. Reference may be made in particular to the work of Congressman Keating, the chairman of a sub-committee of the House Judiciary Committee, and to Congressman Scott who has recently introduced House Resolution 447, which, if adopted, would go far towards resolving the problems as far as the House is concerned. Senator Bush has made similar proposals in the Senate. Although such codes will by no means solve the whole problem, their adoption would be a great step forward.

Before we leave this matter it should be observed that it is of first importance not only that proper procedures should be established but also that there should be appropriate sanctions to make these procedures effective. This is not easy. Probably the most effective sanction in the long run would be a provision which would relieve a witness from any obligation to testify, and thus from any punishment for refusal to testify, when the procedures are not followed. A sanction against the committee or its members is doubtless unrealistic. But the committee should lose its compulsory powers when it does not conduct itself properly.

Finally, it should be emphasized again that responsibility for working out proper procedures for legislative investigations rests upon Congress and its two Houses. Complaints against the President or others outside of Congress are misdirected. Congress has the power to provide proper procedures for legislative investigations. It would strengthen its powers if it would meet this clear responsibility.

The spirit of due process of law, the law of the land, our ancient heritage of liberty, requires that we bring order and fairness into this field which has recently become so chaotic. We have been through struggles of this sort in the past, and justice and liberty have always eventually won out. Indeed we have been strengthened in our liberties by each such struggle. In this connection, I think of a phrase which was used by our late Chief Justice Harlan F. Stone. He referred to "the sober second thought of the community, which is the firm base on which all law must ultimately rest." (Stone, "The Common Law in the United States," 50 *Harv. L. Rev.* 4, 25; 1936.) For myself, I have great faith in the sober second judgment of the people. The immediate reaction of the people, like that of any individual, may be hasty, emotional, irrational, or unsound. But when that phase is past, when we have had a real chance to think through our problems, I have confidence that the people will demand a better standard of conduct in legislative investigations than has been evidenced in the recent past. In making this statement, I want to pay due and deserved respect to the many members of both Houses who have not abused their powers, and have been scrupulous in the exercise of their authority.

Though we live in stirring times, we should not forget that many generations of our ancestors have lived through times which were for them more trying than ours. It was Æneas who heartened his men by saying to them: "Oh you who have lived through worse days . . ." It is not surprising that now, as in earlier times, there have been those who seek to exploit our fears. Nor should it be surprising that many people, at first, at least, respond to such exploitation. But it is the way of life to have to meet new problems; and, while doing so, we should not give up old values.

In protecting ourselves from the threat of communism, we should not adopt methods of oppression here which the communists themselves would use. After all, the essence of communism is the subordination of the individual to the state. And the essence of liberty, for which our ancestors fought on both sides of the Atlantic, is the freedom of the individual from the arbitrary power of governmental authorities. When we see more clearly that our present problem is simply one of due process of law in its pervasive sense, so fundamental throughout more than seven centuries of history, we will have no difficulty in finding a satisfactory solution which will recognize and preserve the basic rights of individuals while providing ample protection for the state.

The problems of our day may be useful problems. It is good, I think, that we should have to bestir ourselves from time to time to protect our liberties, as our ancestors did on many occasions in the past. If we take these rights for granted, if we accept them as a matter of course, we may simply fritter them away, and end by losing them, and possibly deserving to lose them. And so I would suggest that you not be discouraged, nor even be unduly concerned if basic human rights are under attack. These are rights which thrive in vindication, and each generation better understands them and their significance if it has to think them through for itself. We are given a great opportunity today, to which I think we will measure up, if the past is any guide. Like the barons at Runnymede, like Coke and Locke and Otis and Adams and Madison, and many others whose names are lost to fame, we may be able to make our own contribution to that ancient concept which has rallied the spirits of free Englishmen and Americans for many centuries — the law of the land.

3 THE FIFTH AMENDMENT AS A SYMBOL

The provision of the Fifth Amendment that a person need not be a witness against himself has been much with us in recent months. Many people, I suppose, though not prepared to say that the amendment should be done away with, are rather inclined to feel that they have heard enough of it for a while. It has been my lot to think about these problems a good deal over the past several months. A number of earnest and sincere people have written to me, often at some length, and I have considered their arguments carefully. But I have not found anything to change my view that this provision is one of fundamental importance in our legal and social system. Indeed, I have come to feel that it is important not only for itself, but also as a symbol of our best aspirations and our deep-seated sense of justice. I am going to try to develop now some of the reasons which have led me to this conclusion.

In a speech which I made last spring, I outlined some of the history of the Fifth Amendment, both before and after our revolution. I showed how it arose, almost abruptly, out of the great political struggles in England in the seventeenth century. As a part of our common-law heritage it was transplanted to this country, and incorporated into our Constitution with the amendments constituting our Bill of Rights. I stated my view that the privilege against self-incrimination is one of the great landmarks in man's struggle to make himself civilized. There appears to be no reason to withdraw from that conclusion. Indeed, as I have indicated, this appears to me to be only the beginning, only the foundation, of the real importance of the Fifth Amendment.

As in the case of most matters where the emotions and the judgment may not be in immediate accord, it takes a while for judgment to prevail. Judgment on such matters is helped by full consideration and by better understanding. One of my purposes in speaking on this subject lies in the hope that it may contribute to that understanding.

At the outset, a question may naturally be raised, to which reference may be made. The constitutional provision in the Fifth Amendment says that no person shall be required to testify against himself "in any criminal case." Is it not clear that a legislative investigation is not a "criminal case"? What application, then, does the constitutional provision have in such proceedings — or in civil trials, or elsewhere, where persons may be subjected to questioning? This is a question which was raised and answered long ago, so long ago in fact that lawyers tend to take it for granted. But early courts saw that the protection of the amendment itself would be an empty gesture if it was literally applied. For example, if the witness is required to answer self-incriminating questions in a civil trial, or in a legislative investigation, the prosecuting officer can use his answers to provide evidence on which he can be prosecuted or convicted. Even if the prosecuting officer cannot use his testimony itself, he can, from that testimony, learn other facts which he could use in the prosecution. For example, the witness could be asked where he hid the property he stole, or who his associates were. Then the property itself could be located and used at the trial, or the associates could be found and brought in as witnesses against the person who had been required to disclose their identity.

For this reason, courts long ago concluded that if the privilege is to be effective at all it must be given a comprehensive application, and thus must prevent compulsory self-incrimination in *any* proceeding. This is, indeed, a broad construction of the constitutional language, but it is a construction which has seemed to be required if the basic objective of that language is to be realized.

Before I turn to the symbolic importance of the privilege against self-incrimination, I would like to present some further discussion of problems raised by the privilege itself. As is the case with many basic ideas and problems in the field of human relations, the questions raised by the Fifth Amendment are far from clear. Its provisions are among those things we take for granted in ordinary times. Only in times of stress do we really find ourselves devoting thought and effort to the underlying issues. These issues are not fairly represented in terms of black and white. Like all serious problems meriting our close attention, these questions are ones in which there are factors tending both ways. They are questions of degree, and as has been wisely said of such questions, they are none the worse for it. But such questions do require more careful discrimination and analysis than is sometimes given them.

Many people have approached the Fifth Amendment in recent months in a rigid and mechanical way. They say: "A person claiming the privilege against self-incrimination under the Fifth Amendment, or under a similar provision of a state constitution, is guilty or else he is lying. Anyone can see that." They say: "It's as simple as two plus two equals four. There are only two ways. If he claims the privilege honestly, he must fear incrimination, which means that if he answers the question, he must admit that he has committed a crime. And if he claims the privilege dishonestly, of course he is lying, and since he is under oath, he has committed perjury. No other explanation is logically possible." That is what we are often told. And on either basis, the person claiming the privilege has condemned himself, and should be forthwith dismissed from whatever he has been doing, and generally blacklisted and deprived of his livelihood. Indeed, this position has been taken (in entire good faith, I am sure, in a bona fide effort to resolve a problem which I have acknowledged is one of great difficulty) in a number of proceedings.

In my previous speeches I have tried to develop some of the reasons why this conclusion may not be warranted in a particular case. It is not true that there are only two alternatives. A person may fear and honestly fear the risk of prosecution even though he knows he has committed no crime. He is entitled to claim the benefit of the privilege in such a case, and an inference that he has committed a crime is simply wrong. Similarly, I have previously tried to develop the confusing effect of the doctrine of "waiver" of the privilege and the influence it has had in many cases in inducing witnesses not to answer questions of the greatest gravity.

It may well be, as has been said by high authority, that the Fifth Amendment protects against prosecution for crime, but it cannot protect against the obvious inference which would be taken by any thinking person. I would like to suggest again that in many circumstances that inference is not wholly warranted. A person who thinks a little further about the matter may find that there are many factors in some of these situations which must be taken into account before he reaches any conclusion about the inference he should take.

We are often given the example of the bank teller who claims the privilege against incriminating himself when he is asked whether he is the person who stole the missing thousand dollars. We are told that such a bank teller would be immediately dismissed; and doubtless he would be, and very likely with great propriety. This example is often advanced as establishing the proposition that the same result should follow as a matter of course in all other Fifth Amendment cases. It is my purpose now to suggest that it is not as simple as that. The inferences to be drawn and the consequences which should ensue in these cases may well merit our more careful attention and more discriminating thought.

Though I know that this is not put as effectively and clearly as I would like to be able to put it, I am going to try to propose and outline two distinctions which seem to me to be sound and relevant in our consideration of current problems.

The first matter to which I think we should give careful attention in all of these cases is *the nature of the question which is asked* and which the witness refuses to answer under the shelter of the Fifth Amendment. Here again the problem is one of degree. There is no clear and sharply demarcated line. The question whether a bank teller stole funds entrusted to him is one sort of question. But the closer the question asked gets to the area of opinion and political belief, the less significant, I suggest to you, is the refusal to answer questions. Or, to put this another way, the more the interrogation gets into what might be called the free-speech area of the First Amendment, the more difficult it is to come up surely with a sound inference from the refusal to answer a question.

Now, I may well be asked: Isn't a conspiracy to overthrow our government by force and violence, using murder and all the other evil methods that the communists have shown that they are capable of, at least as bad (to put it mildly) as taking a thousand dollars? Of course it is — far worse. But putting the question that way does not help us to advance our thought. The question is not how bad these two things are, but what conduct the person we are considering actually engaged in.

The word "communist" is used with many meanings. Some people automatically jump to the worst meaning. Yet people who have been communists in the past, or who have allowed themselves to be used by communist interests, may in fact have been tempted by the communist lure while holding less sinister motives and intentions. Their approach may have been made, and their actions taken, in terms which were to them purely political and innocent. They were, to be sure, quite wrong, and may well by now long since have concluded that they were wrong.

Now, many years later, with the benefit of much hindsight, we see the activities in which these people engaged in a very unfavorable light. But the persons who engaged in these activities, and who had these associations about which inquiries are currently being made, did not act themselves in that light. To them, the questions which are now asked often relate directly to matters which they consider to be their personal beliefs and political opinions. And they know from what they read in the papers, and from what their counsel tell them, that information which they now give about these past acts and associations can lead to criminal prosecution.

So they claim the privilege. This is of course frustrating to investigating or prosecuting officers. In many cases it is unwise from the point of view of the person who claims the privilege. I wish myself that these people would candidly testify as to what they have done, at least before a proper tribunal or agency. But it is easier to wish that someone else would be a martyr than it is to be one yourself. And the point here is that, under these circumstances, the privilege may be claimed without the person having in fact actually done anything criminal at all.

As I have said, it is a question of degree. I am not trying to give a simple or positive answer. I am trying to point out something that has usually been overlooked in recent considerations of this problem: namely, that there may in fact be no clear or compelling basis for drawing any inference against a person claiming the privilege against self-incrimination when the question he refuses to answer is one which is, or which he feels to be, directed to his opinions or political beliefs. And this has been true of many of the unanswered questions in recent years.

In a proceeding now pending in New Hampshire, a witness has been held in contempt because he refused to answer questions about a lecture he gave, as a guest, at the state University, and because he refused to respond to questions as to his meaning in a certain passage of a translation he had made — a translation, please note — of one of the books of Engels. He did not stand on the Fifth Amendment at all. He did not claim that he would be incriminated by his answer. His position was simply that an American is not to be subjected to questioning by public authority about his opinions or beliefs. If the guarantees of the First Amendment — free speech, free press, free religion — mean anything, and I am sure they do, do they not require protection here? In the New Hampshire case, the issue stands out clearly. I would suggest, however, that in a number of the cases in which the Fifth Amendment has been claimed, the underlying reason, and perhaps the sound reason, is more closely connected with the First Amendment than with the Fifth. In many cases, the Fifth Amendment has been used, perhaps erroneously, as a protection of free speech and free assembly. Where this is the real reason for refusing to answer a question, the inference which might be taken from the refusal may be quite unwarranted.

In this connection, we may well recall the sentence with which Tacitus began his History more than eighteen hundred years ago. "Rare and happy are the times," he wrote, "when we may think what we please, and express what we think." (Tacitus, *The History*, Book I, 1). I have long cherished the deep belief that this is a simple expression of one of the great things for which America stands.

Now I turn to the second factor to which I wish to draw your attention. This too is a question of degree. I am referring to *the nature of the tribunal which subjects the witness to questioning.*

Our courts are for the most part well run. They are presided over by disinterested judges, and are bent on seeking the truth with careful regard for the rights of individuals. They have no axes to grind. They do not move on their own initiative, but only when they are properly invoked. They do not act for their own purposes, but only when they are called upon to do justice. In various ways, through constitutions, through the common law, and through the traditions of the bench and bar, our judges are made, in the language of the Massachusetts Constitution, "as free, impartial, and independent as the lot of humanity will admit."

To a very considerable extent, this is true of administrative agencies and officials. In many areas, high traditions and standards have been developed here. From time to time, Congress has been concerned about the standard of justice maintained by administrative agencies, and statutes have been passed, like the Administrative Procedure Act, to improve that standard. One of the objectives of a number of these statutes is the separating of the prosecuting from the deciding function, and the provision of a measure of independence for the person who is called on to decide.

When we come to legislative investigations, however, we have a wholly different situation. Here, nearly every safeguard which has been developed over the centuries by our courts is thrown out the window. We are told that a legislative committee is not a court, and that court rules do not apply. We are told too that a committee or sub-committee is only conducting an investigation, not a trial, and that Congress or a legislature would be severely hampered in its law-making function if it were bound by cumbersome court rules. The situation is surely different. Indeed, experience has taught us that the risks are very great in legislative investigations, which might suggest that this was a place where even greater safeguards should be imposed. At any rate, none of the reasons given would seem to be an adequate ground for not recognizing that the rights of the individual, established after so long a struggle, are just as precious before a legislative body as they are in court.

It is of course true that most legislators are thoroughly conscientious and competent citizens. And many legislative hearings are properly conducted, and are of great assistance to the legislative body in the formulation of legislation and in the discharge of other legislative responsibilities. But no legislator is as independent as a judge. All legislators are necessarily and naturally engaged in politics. Why do we not recognize as a matter of course that many of the basic safeguards of individual rights are just as important in a legislative investigation as any place else?

A legislative committee conducting an investigation of an explosive problem inevitably is engaged in politics. I do not use that word in any slighting way. Politics is surely one of the most important activities in a democracy. But any person engaged in politics is constantly and naturally concerned about the effect his actions will have in attracting or repelling votes. This is true in the simplest and most carefully conducted proceeding. Now let us consider an investigation which is not so carefully conducted. Let us mix in a large measure of television, newsreels, radio, after-session press releases, and so on. In this atmosphere, why is it not obvious that disinterestedness retreats to the background, and that this is true with respect to many controversial legislative investigations?

Let me make it plain that I am not referring to a single committee, nor to the present time alone. The widely applauded committee which investigated crime some two years ago was a frequent violator. The large number of disapprovals of its actions by the courts which have followed in its wake should be better known. And is there anyone who would say that political considerations were not involved in that committee's actions? Reference may also be made to the committee which recently investigated tax-exempt foundations. After developing the case against the foundations, this committee closed its hearing without giving the foundations a chance to present their defense. Such conduct is hardly calculated to foster confidence in the fairness of committee investigations.

And, as I have indicated, this is not a new or merely

current problem. Without going further into the past, there was much that was wrong about some of the investigations in the 1920's. I have been charged with not having criticized the committees of that time, but I can plead infancy until 1925, and youth for the remaining five years of the decade. I surely have no hesitation in saying now that the actions of committees in that period strengthen my belief that a Congressional committee is not a place where the highest standards of the protection of the individual can always be found. The same conclusion can also be rested on an examination of investigations conducted under the aegis of another party in the 1930's.

It is by no means too much to say that in this whole area history teaches us that this is an old problem. And history and careful analysis together show that it is an inherent problem. By rules and standards and other devices, procedure in legislative investigations can be improved over what we have often seen in recent years. But in legislative investigations of controversial subjects, there will always be great risks that any standards set up will yield or be circumvented in one way or another.

At its best, a legislative investigation is not too satisfactory a place to be concerned with individual rights, nor for creating confidence in the witness that his rights will be safeguarded and respected. As I have said before, I want to make it plain that individual legislators and many committees have shown that they can be scrupulous in their efforts to conduct hearings fairly and well. And many hearings which are not really on controversial matters are conducted well as a matter of course, and we want to be careful not to interfere with the legitimate and necessary right of Congress to get information and opinions which will help it in passing laws and carrying out its other duties.

But at their worst, legislative investigations can be quite unsatisfactory, and we have seen some unfortunate examples in recent years. It has been difficult to get legislative bodies to exercise their collective responsibility in this area. Until very recently, each individual legislator has been pretty much a law unto himself. A committee of the Senate has now made a report with respect to a member of that body, and this deals with one instance of the violation of the rights of a witness. This is an important event. Had it been necessary, however, the committee could have found other fish in the same pond.

I have developed this question at some length; you may think at too great length. But it has to be spelled out I think because these facts have not been wholly clear, and the general public as well as legislative bodies have been loath to accept the facts and their natural consequences. What is the relevance of the inherent nature of the legislative hearing to the matter with which we are concerned?

Let us stop and think a moment about the situation of a witness who comes before a legislative body in a controversial matter. It may be very hard for you to do, but let me ask you to try to put yourself in the place of such a witness. What does a person do when he finds himself summoned before a legislative committee in which he has no confidence? In recent experience, this has often been a one-man sub-committee, where the witness finds presiding a legislator who is judge, jury, prosecutor, castigator, and press agent, all in one. Our witness is not a lawyer. He has not thought these things through in great detail. He has read about the Fifth Amendment in the papers, and he may have received advice about it from his lawyer — and is it not his lawyer's duty to give him such advice? The witness is frightened by the publicity to which he has been subjected, by the TV cameras and lights, by the noise and confusion, and especially by the excesses which he sees before him. He has no confidence in the proceeding. In this situation, he takes refuge in the Fifth Amendment. It will not do, I think, to say that this is not realistic. I suggest to you that this is a fair description of the situation which has confronted many witnesses over the past several years. It is not a matter of which either we as citizens or our legislative bodies can be proud.

In this circumstance, is it sound to take the inference that the man who refuses to answer questions, especially questions as to his past beliefs and opinions, on the ground of self-incrimination, is guilty of something heinous or else is a liar? I do not think that it is. I think that we should give more heed to the nature of the tribunal, and the character (or lack of character) of the proceeding it is conducting, before we decide what weight should be given to a claim of the Fifth Amendment privilege.

Let me make it plain that I am not seeking to lay down any absolutes. I am by no means saying that every witness who claims the Fifth Amendment's privilege is wholly innocent of wrongdoing. Many of them are surely guilty of some offense. All I am trying to say is that the determination of that question is, or may be, an extremely difficult one, and any conclusion which is reached automatically is likely to be a wrong one. In some cases, people have to decide what effect should be given to a claim of privilege. In that situation, careful investigation and consideration of all of the circumstances should be given. At the very least I suggest to you again that (1) the nature of the question asked, and (2) the nature of the tribunal, are matters which merit very careful consideration in evaluating a claim of privilege. There is no necessary relation between the effect which should be given to the bank teller's refusal to answer before a court and the refusal of a witness to answer before a one-man legislative sub-committee a question which the witness believes to relate to his past political beliefs.

Instead of decrying the Fifth Amendment, we may well feel satisfaction at the protection the Amendment has given to individuals standing alone, against abuses which for centuries would never be tolerated in any of our courts. The unfairnesses have by no means been confined to the hearing room. Indeed much of the atmosphere in these matters has been produced by statements, press releases, and speeches made outside of committee hearings. People have often been branded as Fifth-Amendment communists — from which the less thinking portions of the general public conclude at once that it has been established that they are conspiratorial treasonous communists, when there may be no evidence that they are communists at all. Their claim of privilege may in fact be largely a reflection on the kind of hearing to which they have been subjected, and thus in reality something which should bear heavily against those who are branding them as Fifth-Amendment communists.

And then there is another phrase, which seems to me to reach one of the several low points in this whole area. This is the talk of "anti-anti-communists," the cumbersome expression being used as if it was an honest way of describing something bad. Let us look at this concoction for a moment. Note that there is implicit in this dual hyphenation the assumption that any anti-communist must ipso facto not only be good but beyond any sort of criticism. Now that is an assumption that is surely un-American. Nothing in this country is beyond criticism. A thing, an argument, a method, may be anti-communist, and very bad. A method of anti-communism may be wholly contrary to our constitution and to the rights and liberties which we have inherited from our forefathers and which are one of the chief things which distinguish us from the communists today. We will gain nothing in this country if we adopt the methods of the communists to protect ourselves against communists.

It hardly needs to be said that there are many grounds upon which a particular person claiming to be an anti-communist may be opposed. Hitler was an anti-communist, indeed a fanatical anti-communist, and a great many loyal Americans were opposed to Hitler and what he stood for. I am opposed to the methods used by some other anti-communists. It would be my thought that the intended meaning behind the phrase anti-anti-communist is quite unfounded. Americans can well afford to see through this sort of catchword reasoning.

In this connection let me quote a passage from an authoritative study of modern Russia which has just been published. This is *The Soviet Regime* by W. W. Kulski, of Syracuse University. In this new book, he says: "The totalitarian mind accepts all the means which promise the achievement of its ends. A political democrat is ready to compromise some of his ideal ends for the sake of renouncing means which would involve the sacrifice of human lives or freedom. This is the major moral issue dividing any totalitarian, be he Communist or Fascist, from a genuine democrat."

One of our basic difficulties in this whole area has been our seeking after the illusion of certainty and absolute security. We have been frightened, badly and understandably frightened, by communism. We have been frightened by an internal communist menace as well as by a threat from beyond our borders. Indeed the internal menace has been closer home and has to some seemed more real, and, I suppose, more capable of being actually dealt with. We have, I fear, allowed our concern with the internal threat, which I would not deny, to obscure the fact that the external threat is far more serious. Indeed, one of the great tragedies of recent events, I believe, is the fact that some of the things that have happened in our more ponderous attempts to deal with the internal communist menace have greatly handicapped us in our efforts to build up our greatest defense to the threat abroad. Unless we are to stand alone, we must rally the free world to our side. Great efforts to that end have surely been undercut by a lack of confidence which our friends have developed in us, based very considerably on events which have occurred in the pursuit of local communists.

Because we have been frightened, we have succumbed too readily to the thought that communism could be wholly stamped out at home, and that the way to do it was to stamp, and to stamp without too much concern lest some of the stamping not be confined to communists. Should it not be clear to us, though, that this quest for certainty, for complete protection, is the pursuit of an illusion? The human mind in many situations often seeks the satisfaction of certainty. Is this not a matter, though, in which we must constantly strive to balance competing considerations? Former Ambassador George F. Kennan, who surely knows much about the Russians and about communism, said in his recent address on "The Illusion of Security":

"What we have to do is not to secure a total absence of danger but to balance peril against peril and to find the tolerable degree of each. . . . a ruthless, reckless insistence on attempting to stamp out everything that could conceivably constitute a reflection of improper foreign influence in our national life, regardless of the actual damage it is doing or the cost of eliminating it, in terms of other American values, is the one thing I can think of that could reduce us all to a point where the very independence we are seeking to defend would be meaningless, for we would be doing things to ourselves as vicious and tyrannical as any that might be brought to us from outside."

And there is another passage in that speech which seems to me to be worthy of our consideration as we examine these problems:

"In this personal existence of ours, bounded as it is at both ends by suffering and uncertainty, and constantly attended by the possibility of illness and accident and tragedy, total security is likewise a myth. Here, too, an anxious perfectionism can operate to destroy those real underpinnings of existence, founded in faith, modesty, humor, and a sense of relativity, on which alone a tolerable human existence can be built. The first criterion of a healthy spirit is the ability to walk cheerfully and sensibly amid the congenital uncertainties of existence, to recognize as natural the inevitable precariousness of the human condition, to accept this without being disoriented by it, and to live effectively and usefully in its shadow."

When we recognize that we cannot achieve absolute security, when we recognize that there are other values to preserve while we are fighting communism if we are not to lose the very things we seek to protect when we oppose communism, then we can see the Fifth Amendment in a new perspective. I believe the Fifth Amendment is, and has been through this period of crisis, an expression of the moral striving of the community. It has been a reflection of our common conscience, a symbol of the America which stirs our hearts.

The Fifth Amendment has been very nearly a lone sure rock in a time of storm. It has been one thing which has held quite firm, although something like a juggernaut has pushed upon it. It has, thus, through all its vicissitudes, been a symbol of the ultimate moral sense of the community, upholding the best in us, when otherwise there was a good deal of wavering under the pressures of the times.

The great contributions which have been made in recent months by such persons as, in the first instance, Joseph N. Welch, and later, Senator Watkins and his associates, have been, I believe, the mobilization of the moral sense of the nation to bear upon a related problem. That sense is often latent. It is deeply felt and tenaciously maintained; but it is not easily aroused. We do not in this nation wear our morals on our sleeve. They tend to be a personal matter, and though there may be a great common moral feeling, it is often not easy to bring it to bear upon a difficult problem. But these issues are, to a considerable extent, in last analysis moral issues. And we are a nation that is essentially moral. The Fifth Amendment has played a part in the process of crystallizing our moral sense. It has been a symbol of our moral striving, of our sense of the essential importance and dignity of the individual.

Let me read you a few words from a talk made by Mr. Welch at a recent meeting of Harvard Law School graduates in Chicago:

"It seems to me that we are measuring our reactions in this country certainly by our emotions and not by logic or reason. . . . The two principal emotions now in evidence in this country in the area where I was acting are fear and hate, and fear and hate when fanned to a white heat are frightening to me, and anyone who fans these emotions to a white heat, I think, may be doing this country a disservice. . . . It is not necessary for us to live in a steady atmosphere of fright and terror. It is not necessary for us to hate as much as it seems to me we do. I have always thought hatred a bad diet, and I must say that I think a steady and prolonged diet of fear and hate might well destroy us. . . . It seems to me that in this lovely land of ours there is no problem we cannot solve, no menace we cannot meet, nor is it in any sense necessary that we either surrender or impair any of our ancient, beautiful freedoms."

One way to evaluate a political instrument is to consider what the situation would be if it did not exist. We may better understand the importance of the Fifth Amendment by considering what not having it would mean. We usually think of the privilege against self-incrimination either in historical terms, in the light of past tyrannies, or in terms of the embarrassment that a witness at a Congressional hearing may experience as a result of the exposure of political mistakes. Let us look, though, at the reverse side of the coin in terms of the standard operating procedures of the police states which have brought the medieval techniques up to date. If we are not willing to let the Amendment be invoked, where, over time, are we going to stop when police, prosecutors, or chairmen want to get people to talk? Lurking in the background here are really ugly dangers which might transform our whole system of free government. In this light, the frustrations caused by the Amendment are a small price to pay for the fundamental protection it provides.

One of the functions of government, based on long experience, is at times to protect the citizen against the government. This function has been performed, to some extent, by the Fifth Amendment, although not always perfectly, and not always without some loss to legitimate government interests. While protecting the citizen against the government, the Fifth Amendment has been a firm reminder of the importance of the individual.

Our approach to the Fifth Amendment need not be wholly in terms of defending and explaining it. We may also utilize it, in a sense, offensively, as a reminder of the necessity of maintaining constant vigilance for the protection of individual rights. As a symbol, the Fifth Amendment can be a guide to a number of things which we should be doing better, and which we as members of the bar might well be doing more to improve.

Let me outline five points where present practices in the safeguarding of individual rights and liberties often seem to me to leave much to be desired.

1. It has been said by people in a position to know that probably most of the violations of civil rights in this country are committed by the police. Police officers have a difficult task to perform, and they are subject to great pressures in their important work of protecting the community. We have done little that is effective towards developing and maintaining proper standards for the conduct of this work. "Third degree" cases are constantly in the courts. Some twenty-five years ago, an extensive survey was made of this problem under the auspices of the National Commission on Law Observance and Law Enforcement. The report which resulted was not encouraging. It is difficult to see, though, any im-

provements which have been made in this area since that time. Most of us simply shrug the problem off, and feel that there is little that can be done about it.

There is need for better standards and practices here, and we ought to be doing something about it.

2. Another problem comes a little farther along the chronological line. In a good many states, including my own, prosecuting officers are much too free, it seems to me, in making statements to the press in advance of trial. We are often told that a person has confessed. Sometimes, the full text of a confession is printed in the papers, full of lurid details. Sometimes prosecuting officers issue statements or give interviews in which the case is discussed in detail. This seems to me to be not only an impropriety, contrary to the ancient traditions of the bar, but also wholly unfair to the defendant who is entitled to a fair trial in court without a pre-trial in the newspapers. But, in recent times at least, have disciplinary actions ever been taken in such cases? Do our bar associations pay any attention to it at all? I have seen no evidence that they do. It may merit their more careful attention.

3. Next we come to the reporting of the actual trials in criminal cases. This is a difficult and delicate question. Nevertheless it is an important one, and should not be allowed to go by default as it generally has in the past. Of course, we encounter here another principle of great importance, the freedom of the press. But all freedoms carry with them responsibilities; and the press should exercise more responsibility in this area than it has in this

country in the past. If the press is unable to work out a way to meet this responsibility, then it should be given some help. As you know, the rules on this matter are very strict in England (and in Canada, too, for that matter), yet no one would say for a moment that England and Canada do not have a free press, indeed a press as free as ours.

In this connection, there is a practice that seems to me to be particularly reprehensible, as to which the basic responsibility lies with lawyers rather than with the press. I am referring to the release of evidence to the newspapers. Sometimes this is an advance statement of what the evidence will be. In other cases it is evidence which has been excluded at the trial. It has been known that the jurors in a case read in the newspapers the evidence which the judge excluded from their consideration at the trial itself. Where such practices occur it should be possible to deal with them by the court or through the bar association. Yet I have never heard of a bar association taking action in such a case.

4. Now we come to another matter. Although our constitutions generally guarantee a defendant the right to be represented by counsel, we often do very little to see that that right is made effective. Many defendants in criminal cases do not have the means to retain competent counsel. In a great many states, including my own, the provisions for providing counsel in such cases are wholly inadequate. The Supreme Court of the United States has been moving slowly towards a rule that counsel

must be furnished, but it has not prescribed such a rule for the states as yet.

But is it not shocking that a person can be charged and tried for burglary or robbery or rape without having the assistance of counsel to advise him and to see that his rights are properly safeguarded, and that what can be said for him is said to court and jury? In a few cities legal aid societies participate in some criminal cases. In a few other cities, there are voluntary defender organizations. In a few states, provision is made for a Public Defender. In still other cases, competent counsel are assigned in the more serious cases, while often nothing is done for many others.

Although the problem probably requires legislative solution, this matter is obviously one that is the responsibility of the bar. The bar should be doing more to help to meet that responsibility.

5. Another area in which we have, I feel, failed to live up to our best ideals of the rights of individuals is in the conduct of certain types of trials. Although I am not one who thinks that informers should never be used, there has recently been some rather undiscriminating use of informers. Particularly in loyalty and in immigration cases, and in such matters as the granting of passports and visas, secret evidence is utilized, often from persons unknown to the person who is making the decision. Lack of confrontation has become common practice in these cases. We have done many things in these areas of which we will not be proud in days to come, I verily believe.

We have had to deal with difficult problems in this area, and it may not be surprising if we did not immediately develop adequate procedures. But the time has now come when we should do better than we have been doing. This country was built on individual liberty. It will never be saved in the long run by submerging individual rights in the quest for absolute safety for the state.

There is another matter in connection with the Fifth Amendment which merits careful attention but which is too large to deal with here. I am referring to the granting of immunity from prosecution to a witness as a means of requiring him to testify despite the constitutional privilege. Such statutes are not novel. They have been used in both the state and federal fields for many years. The Compulsory Testimony Act which was recently passed by Congress and became law on August 20, 1954, provides that on the application of the Attorney General or a Congressional Committee a United States District Court may order a witness to testify after his claim of privilege. It then provides that after he has given such testimony, he cannot be prosecuted for any matter covered by his required answers.

This statute gives a protection against prosecution, and thus meets the literal objective of the constitution. Nevertheless, because I attach so much importance to the Fifth Amendment and the values which it symbolizes, I look with misgivings upon this statute. Experience may well show that my doubts are mistaken. I do not think, though, that we should take the present Act for granted, or as the final word in this area. Its actual operation should be carefully observed and objectively appraised.

In considering these problems, the Fifth Amendment can serve as a constant reminder of the high standards set by the Founding Fathers, based on their experience with tyranny. It is an ever-present reminder of our belief in the importance of the individual, a symbol of our highest aspirations. As such it is a clear and eloquent expression of our basic opposition to collectivism, to the unlimited power of the state. It would never be allowed by communists, and thus it may well be regarded as one of the signs which sets us off from communism.

I believe deeply in America and the American people. They have weathered many storms in the past. I am proud of the part that lawyers have played in bringing them through these storms. In times like these, we may well recall an earlier time of stress. One of the great episodes in the history of the American bar came at a relatively early date, when two young lawyers, John Adams and Josiah Quincy, Jr., defended Captain Russell and the British soldiers who had participated in the Boston Massacre. They responded to a call for their services in this cause, though they were recognized patriots, because they felt that the liberty of every man requires that any person charged with crime be able to present his defense as well as possible. The history of the bar is studded with similar acts of courage, in modern times as well as in the past. This is the sort of courage that helps to make a great nation. The bar is slow to move, but it is usually staunch. Let us never forget the great tradition of individual liberty in this country. There are few clearer symbols of this tradition than the Fifth Amendment.

Bei Fragen zur Produktsicherheit wenden Sie sich bitte an:
If you have any questions regarding product safety,
please contact:

Walter de Gruyter GmbH
Genthiner Straße 13
10785 Berlin
productsafety@degruyterbrill.com